Made in the USA
Las Vegas, NV
08 March 2022

45241739R00057